INTERMED CROSSWORDS

for learners of English as a foreign language

by Jonathan Crowther

compiler of crossword puzzles
for *The Observer*

Tokyo
OXFORD UNIVERSITY PRESS
Oxford New York

Oxford University Press
Oxford   New York   Toronto
Delhi   Bombay   Calcutta   Madras   Karachi
Kuala Lumpur   Singapore   Hong Kong   Tokyo
Nairobi   Dar es Salaam   Cape Town
Melbourne   Auckland   Madrid
and associated companies in
Berlin   Ibadan

OXFORD and OXFORD ENGLISH are trade marks of
Oxford University Press

ISBN 0-19-581751-6

Illustrated by Miho Miyazaki

Printing (last digit):
23   24   25   26   27   28   29   30

Printed in Hong Kong
by Calay Printing Co.
Published by Oxford University Press K.K.
2−4−8 Kanamecho, Toshima-ku
Tokyo 171

Preface

This is the third of four graded books of crossword puzzles written especially for learners of English as a foreign language. It is suitable for pupils who have been studying English for three or four years, and introduces about 300 new words not found in the first two (*Introductory* and *Elementary*) books. Further practice is also given with many of the words that do appear in the earlier books. A list of all the words used in the puzzles in this book appears on page 41.

Each clue begins with a number. This shows the number of the square in the diagram where the answer begins. The answers to Across ⇨ clues go from left to right; the answers to **Down** ⇩ clues go from top to bottom.

There are three kinds of clue: (i) pictures, which the pupil must identify and name; (ii) definitions, or descriptions in words of the answers required; (iii) grammatical structures, in which the missing words must be supplied. Occasionally a clue will be of more than one of these kinds.

Across → 1

1 There are fish in it.
3 A kind of flower.
5 (*See picture*.)
9 I am Mary's mother. She is my _____.
11 (*See picture*.)
12 What I buy in the shop I must _____ for.

5 ⇨

Down ↓

1 Next after first.
2 Turkey is in _____.
3 (*See picture*.)
4 When we are ill we _____ in bed.
6 Almost but not quite.
7 (*See picture*.)
8 'Don't do that! _____ doing it!'
10 Put a question.

11 ⇨

3 ⇩   7 ⇩

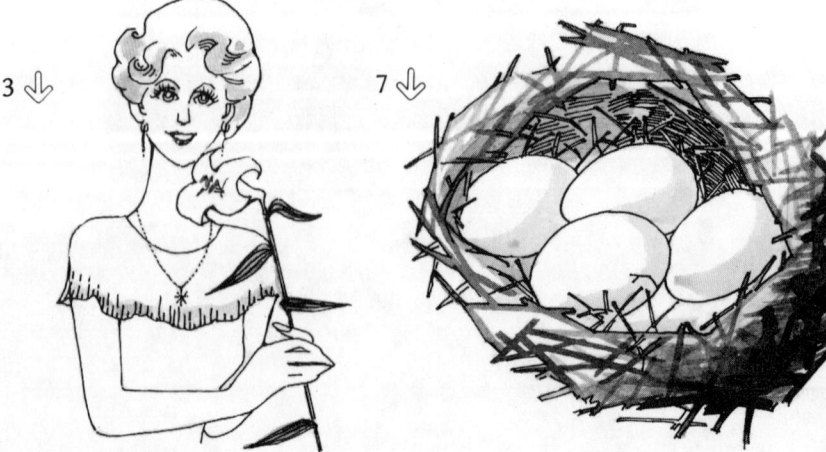

Across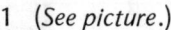

1 (*See picture*.)
3 (*See picture*.)
5 (*See picture*.)
7 (*See picture*.)
8 Sixty minutes make one _____.
9 Will you _____ me tomorrow after school?
11 Give someone something to eat.
13 (*See picture*.)
14 If you hit me with a stick, it will _____.
15 These two hats are almost the same. They are very _____ each other. (*See also picture*.)

Down ↓

1 (*See picture*.)
2 (*See picture*.)
3 My brother and I _____ go to the same school.
4 What did you get for _____ birthday?
5 (*See picture*.)
6 (*See picture*.)
9 I like fishing very _____!
10 What's _____ noise?
11 Susan _____ down and cut her knee.
12 Have you _____ your homework yet?

1 ⇒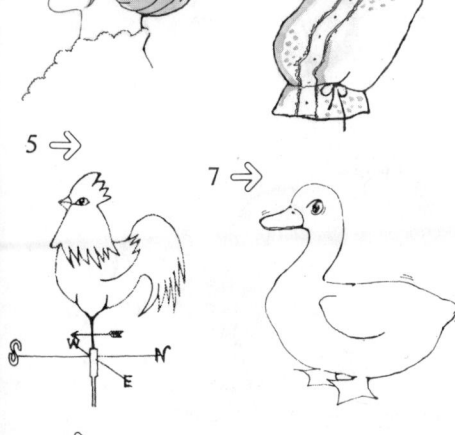

3 ⇒

5 ⇒

7 ⇒

13 ⇒

15 ⇒

5 ⇓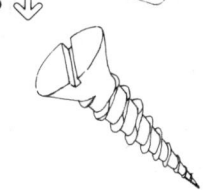

1 ⇓

2 ⇓

6 ⇓

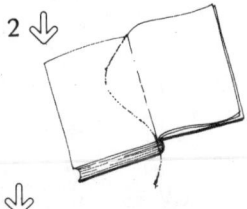

Across →

1 A very big country.
7 I am sick in bed. I am _____.
8 Will John _____ the ball? (*See also picture*.)
9 What flower is this? (*See also picture*.)
10 _____ was this baby born?
13 Not wrong.
15 Move quickly on foot.
16 You'll find them in books.

Down ↓

2 My school is three _____ away.
3 Not poor.
4 (*See picture*.)
5 It has many books in it.
6 What is 12↓ doing?
11 (*See picture*.)
12 (*See picture*—see 6↓.)
14 Each year we _____ older.

	1	2		3		4	
5							6
7				8			
9					10	11	
				12			
13		14			15		
	16						

4 ↓

8 ⇒

11 ↓

9 ⇒

12 ↓

Across →

1. (*See picture.*)
4. It comes out of wells sometimes. This is an ____ well. (*See also picture.*)
5. Bill is kind. He ____ me money sometimes.
7. What is this man reading? (*See also picture.*)
9. (*See picture.*)
11. I have no food. I haven't ____ food.
12. What colour is grass?

4

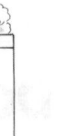

Down ↓

1. Under.
2. (*See picture.*)
3. The ____ is shining. (*See also picture.*)
4. This is my house. I am its ____.
6. I'm ____ that I made you angry.
8. Open, flat land.
10. (*See picture.*)

1 ⇒

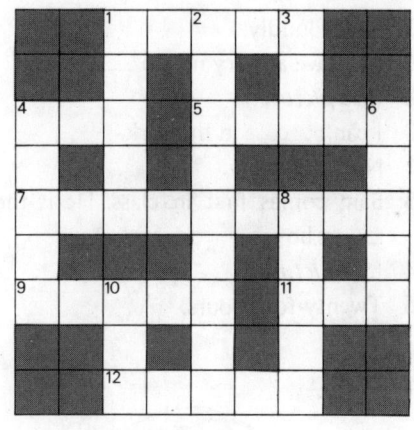

4 ⇒

7 ⇒

2 ⇓

9 ⇒

3 ⇓

10 ⇓

Across →

3 Speak loudly.
6 Be brave and try not to _____.
8 (*See picture*.)
10 I can't _____ in the dark.
11 Not very many.
13 Sam comes first in class. He is the _____ boy.
14 (*See picture*.)
15 Twenty-four hours.

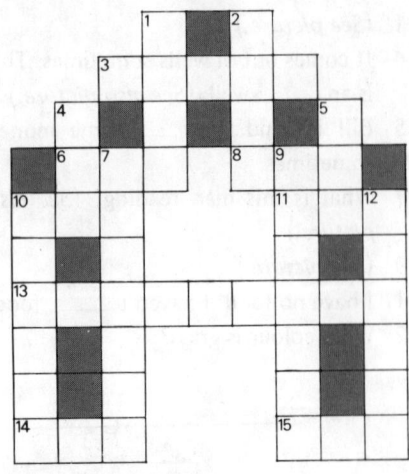

8 ⇨

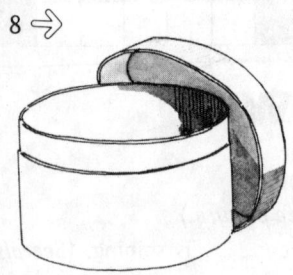

14 ⇨

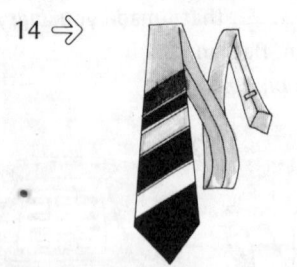

Down ↓

1 I can't find my clothes. Where are _____?
2 Not able to speak.
4 (*See picture*.)
5 (*See picture*.)
7 When will I _____ a letter from you?
9 Ben kindly _____ the old lady his seat.
10 I won't tell you. It's a _____.
12 Rather wet.

4 ⬇

5 ⬇

6

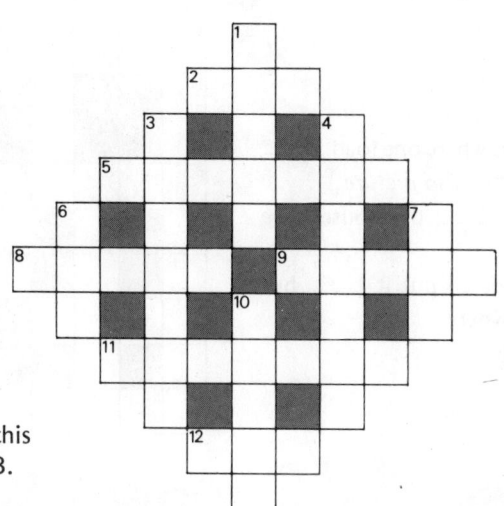

All the answers in this puzzle begin with B.

Across →

2 I'm going to the shops to _____ some fruit.
5 (*See picture*.)
8 When the sun went in, it _____ to rain.
9 (*See picture*.)
11 These are wheel _____. (*See also picture*.)
12 Place where the seashore curves inwards.

Down ↓

1 Make a house or a wall.
3 (*See picture*.)
4 I lend Peter money. He _____ it from me.
6 Ask for money when you are very poor.
7 Not good.
10 This road is not narrow. It is _____. (*See also picture*.)

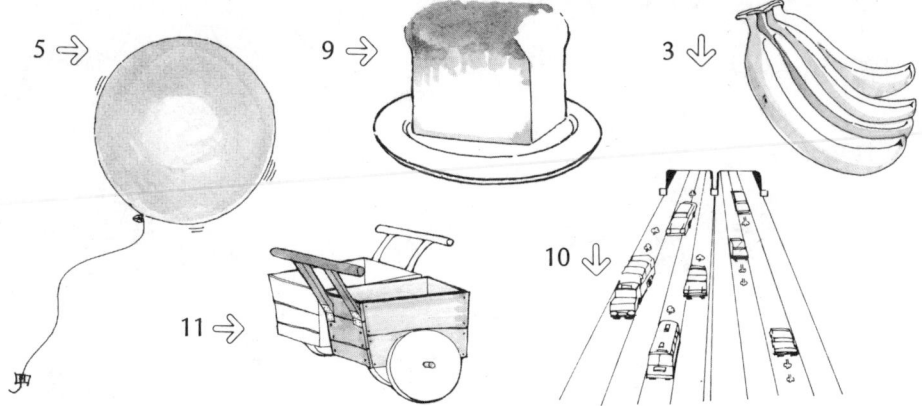

5 ⇨ 9 ⇨ 3 ⬇ 11 ⇨ 10 ⬇

7

Across →

1 (*See picture.*)
5 (*See picture.*)
6 (*See picture.*)
9 This sign shows where one road _____ another one. (*See also picture.*)
11 Bess is going _____ the house. (*See also picture.*)
12 I've lost my coat. I put it _____ but I don't know where.

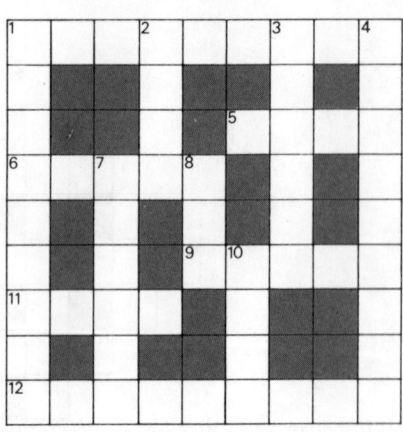

1 ⇨

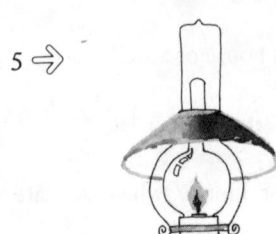
5 ⇨

Down ↓

1 (*See picture.*)
2 Certain.
3 A fast runner has a good _____ of winning the race.
4 I can't buy that book. It's too _____.
7. Way of doing things. A big city needs a good traffic _____.
8 This is a _____. (*See also picture.*)
10 These peaches are 20 pence _____. (*See also picture.*)

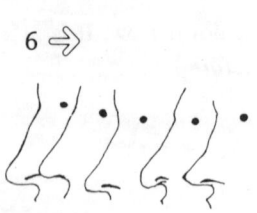
6 ⇨

9 ⇨

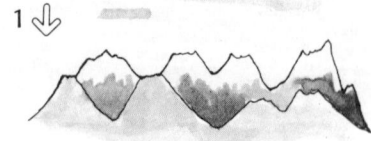
1 ⇩

11 ⇨

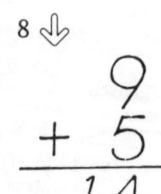
8 ⇩

10 ⇩

8

Across →

3 You send letters by _____. (*See also picture*.)
4 First wash your hands and _____ you can eat.
5 This man looks very _____. (*See also picture*.)
10 The head of a business firm.
11 Try to tell someone what you mean.
12 Please read me a _____.
13 (*See picture*.)
14 Our bodies are covered with _____.

Down ↓

1 This box is _____. (*See also picture*.)
2 (*See picture*.)
6 This month is June. _____ month will be July.
7 'You must not eat in class,' said the teacher. 'That is the _____.'
8 Not slow.
9 Not far away.
10 If you do something wrong you make a _____.
12 I have no more money. I have _____ it all.

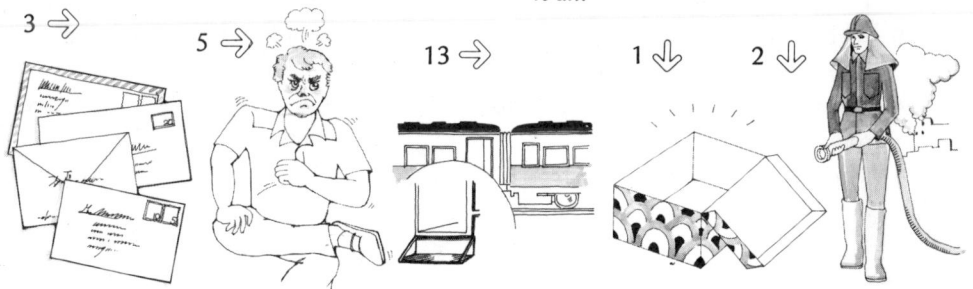

3 ⇒   5 ⇒   13 ⇒   1 ⬇   2 ⬇

9

Across →

1 This man is very _____ . (*See also picture*.)
4 A _____ of toothpaste. (*See also picture*.)
6 Places where a lot of people live.
9 Please _____ to my letter soon.
11 I can't see you today, but I can any _____ day.
12 You _____ me the money I lent you.
13 (*See picture*.)
14 (*See picture*.)
16 This is Jack's ball. It is _____ .
18 Flat, not going up or down.
19 A very young person.
21 When we are not awake, we _____ .
24 When you don't have to pay for something, it is _____ .
25 (*See picture*.)

Down ↓

2 (*See picture*.)
3 Not old.
4 Let's climb to the _____ of the hill.
5 (*See picture*.)
7 Don't wait. Do it _____ !
8 Oh dear, I've _____ on a beetle.
9 When he _____ home, Ben sits down to read.
10 To _____ is human, to forgive divine.
15 My plate's empty. I've eaten it _____ .
17 If you're _____ , I'll ask the doctor to come.
19 (*See picture*.)
20 Very cold water turns into _____ .
22 (*See picture*.)
23 This cat is Aunt Sarah's _____ . (*See also picture*.)

10

1 ⇒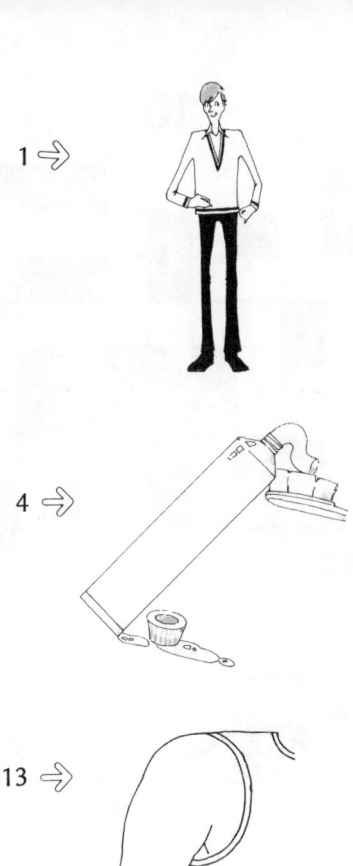

2 ⇓

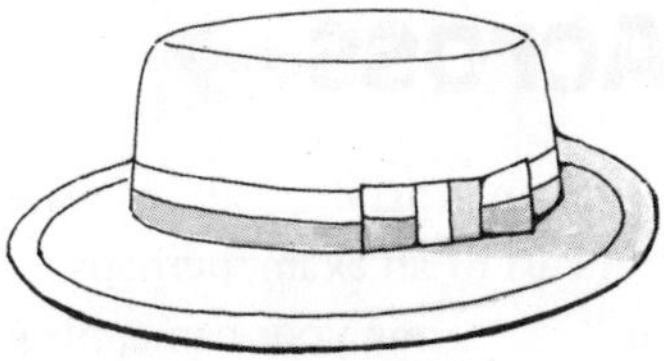

5 ⇓

4 ⇒

19 ⇓

13 ⇒

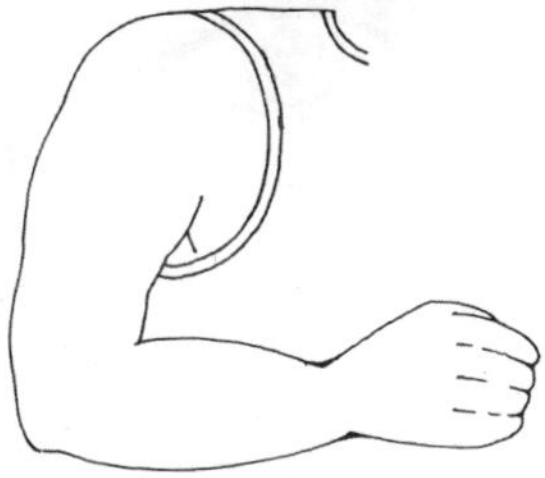

22 ⇓

14 ⇒

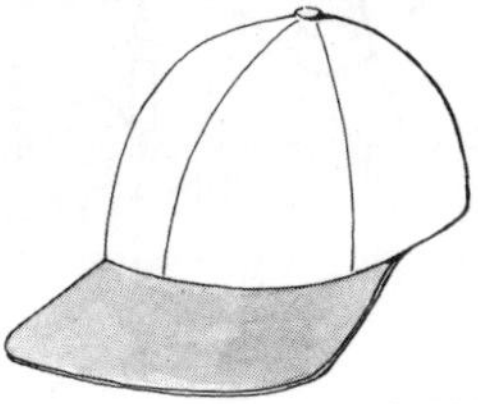

23 ⇓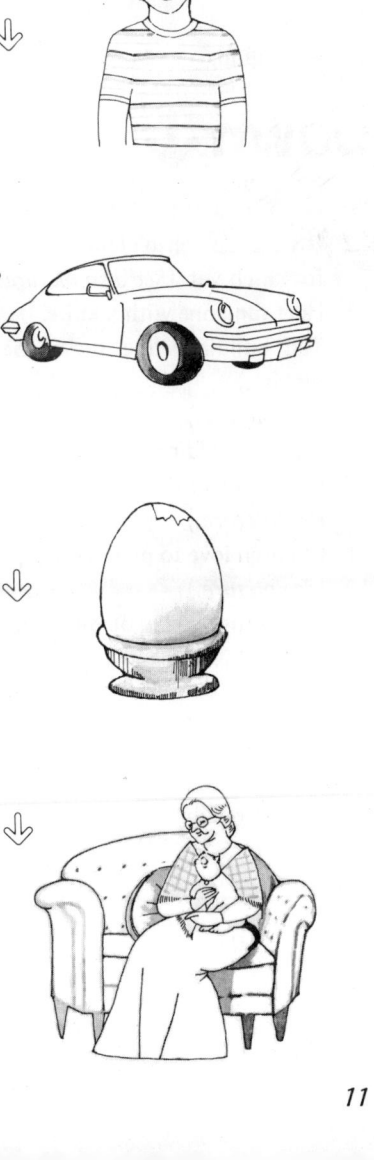

25 ⇒

Across →

10

1 Rain is little _____ of water.
4 Part of an exam, perhaps.
6 _____ me your name, please.
8 (*See picture.*)
10 The black squares in this puzzle make a _____ .
13 Susan and Sally are twins. Their _____ are the same.
15 Neat.
16 Not liquid.

Down ↓

1 At the end of life we _____ .
2 It's _____ ten o'clock. It's not time for lunch yet. (*See also picture.*)
3 Hurt someone with a knife.
5 Tall buildings like these. (*See also picture.*)
6 (*See picture.*)
7 Harry is holding up his _____ hand. (*See also picture.*)
9 (*See picture.*)
11 Children love to play with _____ .
12 (*See picture.*)
14 This is the _____ of this puzzle!

8 →

2 ↓

5 ↓

6 ↓

7 ↓

9 ↓

12 ↓

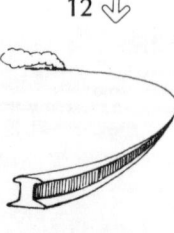

11

All the answers in this
puzzle begin with the same letter.

Across →

2 (*See picture.*)
5 If you cut yourself, it's very _____ .
8 (*See picture.*)
9 Joanna is beautiful, but Jean is _____ .
(*See also picture.*)
11 Mr Jones is _____ at the newspaper.
(*See also picture.*)
12 Don't _____ the wrong word in
here!

Down ↓

1 (*See picture.*)
3 Big, rich houses where kings and
queens live.
4 The horse is _____ the cart. (*See
also picture.*)
6 (*See picture.*)
7 (*See picture.*)
10 Pleased with yourself.

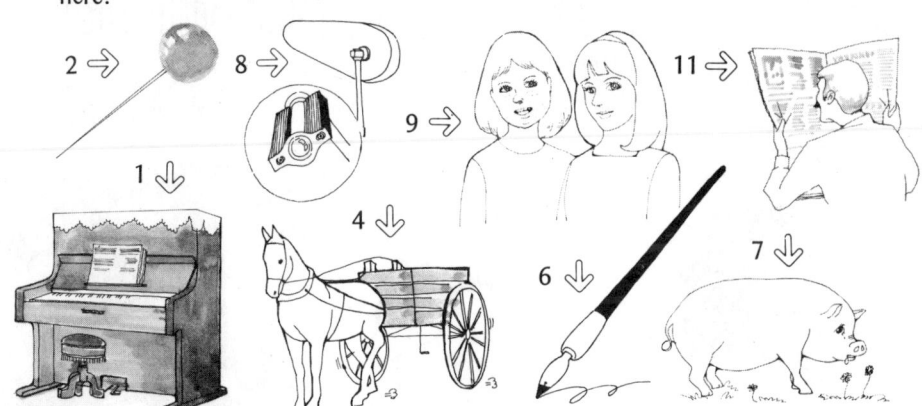

Across →

1 She does typing in an office.
6 Can we play football _____ school?
7 What a silly _____ he is! (*See also picture*.)
8 (*See picture*.)
10 Come _____ . I want to talk to you.
12 (*See picture*.)
13 Made a note of something.
15 All the people.

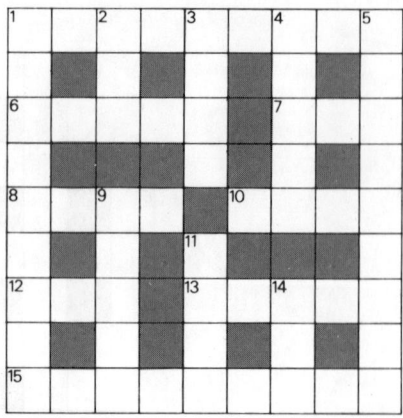

Down ↓

1 (*See picture*.)
2 The baby is sleeping in his _____ . (*See also picture*.)
3 How much money does your father _____ ?
4 Not sleeping.
5 Today is Tuesday. _____ was Monday.
9 Name of a book.
11 Mark's paper is all _____ ! (*See also picture*.)
14 2.

1 ⇓
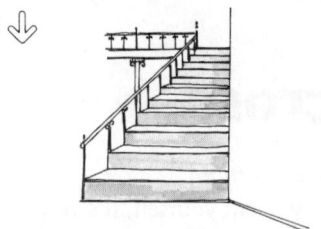

2 ⇓
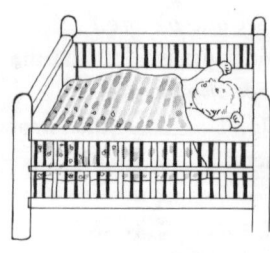

7 ⇒

8 ⇒

12 ⇒

11 ⇓

Across ➜

5 _____ are when men and women get married.
6 Cows and sheep are kept on a _____ .
7 (See picture.)
8 Flowers _____ in the garden.
10 This pin is straight. This one is _____ . (See also picture.)
11 They play games like football and golf.

7 ➩

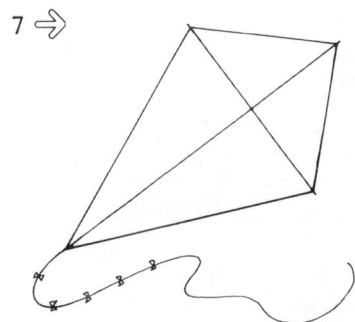

Down ⬇

1 Some 4⬇ in a book may make a _____ .
2 (See picture.)
3 In the day, it's light. At night it's _____ .
4 In writing they start with a capital letter and end with a full stop.
9 (See picture.)
10 John swims well. Peter swims better. But Dick swims _____ of all.

10 ➩

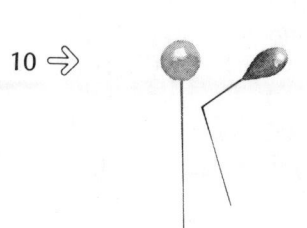

2 ⬇

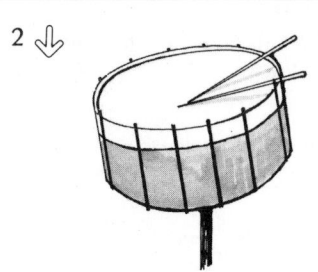

9 ⬇

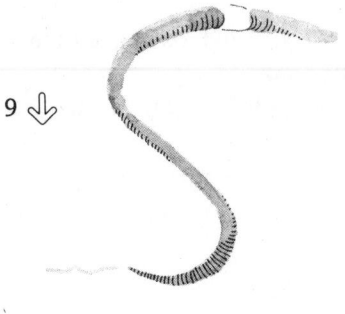

14

All the answers in this puzzle begin with S.

Across →

3 (*See picture.*)
4 (*See picture.*)
5 The army is for soldiers, and the navy is for _____ .
6 Please _____ me a letter soon.
8 A small hut.
10 Children like eating _____ after meals.
12 To turn round and round like a top.
13 A little drink.
14 Margaret goes to school. She is a _____ .
15 A tiny thing that grows into a plant.
16 This is a _____ of water. (*See also picture.*)

Down ↓

1 (*See picture.*)
2 (*See picture.*)
3 When roads are wet or icy, cars often _____ .
4 (*See picture.*)
5 Bill's eyes are closed. He _____ nothing.
6 Be quiet!
7 Farmers _____ us with corn and vegetables.
9 There are sixty _____ in a minute.
11 This is made of _____ . (*See also picture.*)
12 All the children in school call their teacher ' _____ '.
13 Foolish.

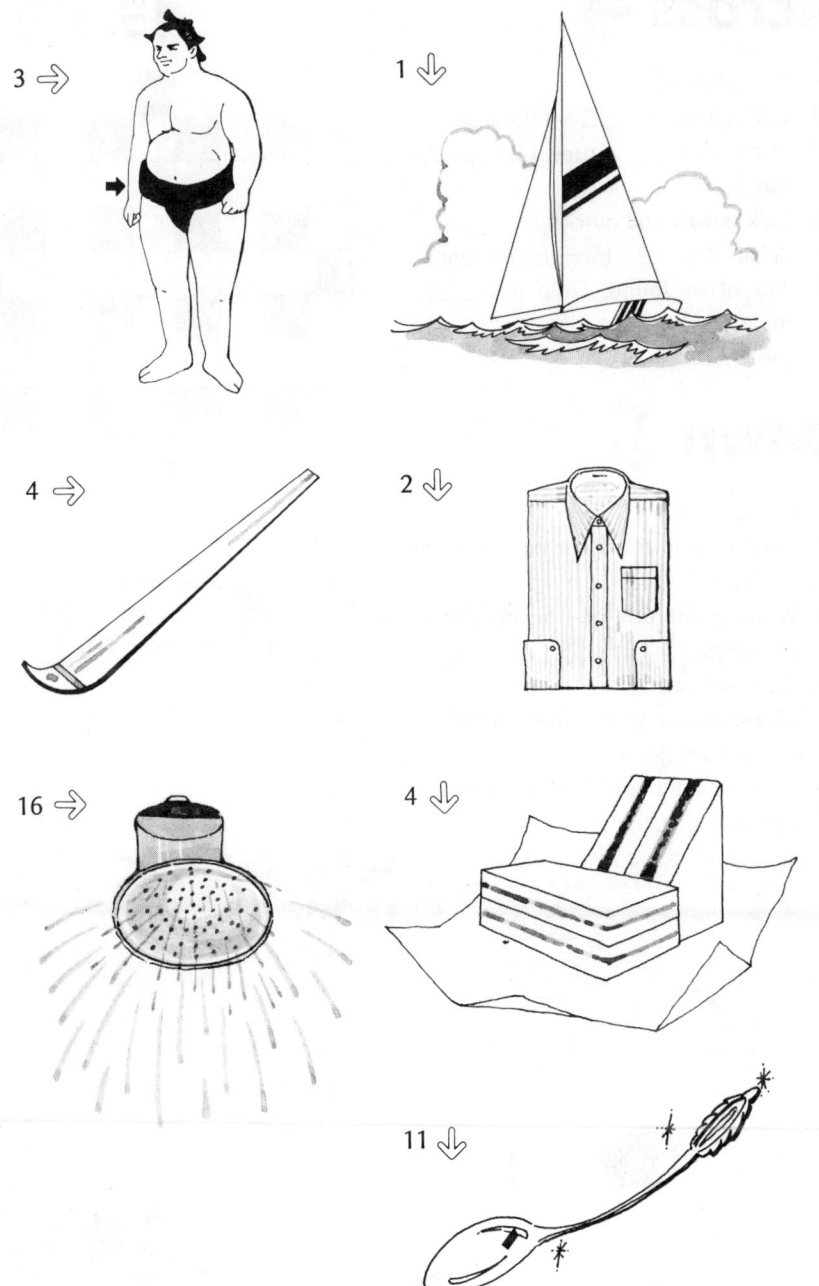

3 ⇒

1 ⇓

4 ⇒

2 ⇓

16 ⇒

4 ⇓

11 ⇓

Across →

15

1 (*See picture.*)
3 Let's go for a _____ in the sea!
7 Harry is _____ a tune. (*See also picture.*)
8 Talk noisily and quickly.
11 A bar of _____ . (*See also picture.*)
12 Not often found. Gold is a _____ metal.
13 (*See picture.*)

Down ↓

1 (*See picture.*)
2 Peter lives in the house next to mine. He is my _____ .
4 White paint put on the outside of buildings.
5 (*See picture.*)
6 Where do you go to catch a train?
9 (*See picture.*)
10 If you find a coin in the street, you can _____ it.

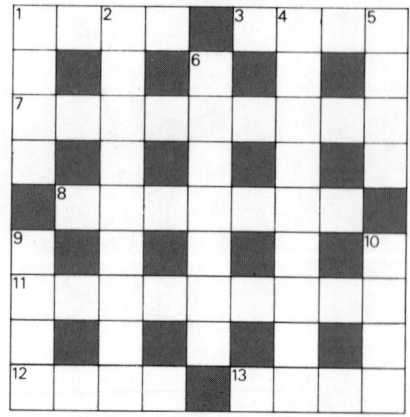

1 ⇓

5 ⇓

1 ⇒

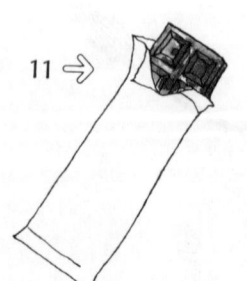

7 ⇒

9 ⇓

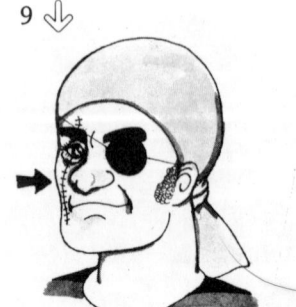

11 ⇒

13 ⇒

Across →

5 Title of a nobleman.
6 This girl's _____ is Anne. (*See also picture.*)
7 My father's father is my _____ .
11 (*See picture.*)
12 This sign is _____ a car. (*See also picture.*)
16 There's a dirty _____ on your face.
17 (*See picture.*)

Down ↓

1 (*See picture.*)
2 The _____ of this square is one square centimetre. (*See also picture.*)
3 If your hands are dirty, _____ them.
4 Does he _____ a hat?
8 Don't make such a _____ ! You'll wake the baby!
9 The car is at the _____ of the house. (*See also picture.*)
10 Jobs of work you have to do.
12 My brother's a soldier in the _____ .
13 Thank you _____ much indeed!
14 I've lost my way. I've no _____ where I am.
15 What do you think this ring is made of? (*See also picture.*)

6 ⇨   11 ⇨   12 ⇨   17 ⇨

1 ⇩   2 ⇩   9 ⇩   15 ⇩

17

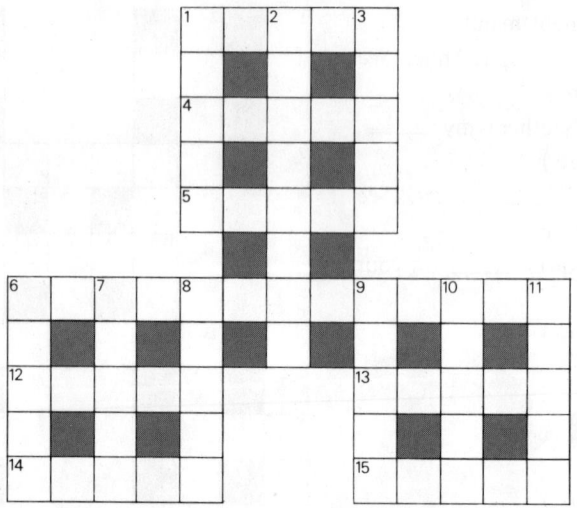

Across →

1   What is the colour of coffee?
4   This plum is still green, but this one is a bit _____ .
5   Do you like the _____ of mint?
6   These puzzles help your _____ of English.
12 (*See picture.*)
13 Martin is eating ice _____ . (*See also picture.*)
14 He is not my friend. He is my _____ .
15 This shop _____ meat. (*See also picture.*)

Down ↓

1   The balloon will soon _____ . (*See also picture.*)
2   Bad is the _____ of good.
3   (*See picture.*)
6   My mother's brother is my _____ .
7   Yesterday my father _____ his new car.
8   If iron gets wet, it becomes _____ .
9   (*See picture.*)
10 The very best. That's an _____ present for Fiona.
11 Football and tennis are _____ .

12 ⇒

13 ⇒

15 ⇒

1 ⇓

3 ⇓

9 ⇓

18

Across →

2 This is a _____ pot. (*See also picture*.)
4 (*See picture*.)
6 Harriet is not _____ tall _____ Marian.
9 Did a sum like 4 + 7.
11 Beat someone in a fight or a game.
14 I don't want this food. Please take _____ away.
15 I am your father. You are _____ son.
16 (*See picture*.)
17 What are we _____ to do tomorrow?
18 The cat is sitting _____ the chair. (*See also picture*.)
19 Someone who shows you the way.
22 K.p.h. stands for 'kilometres _____ hour'.

Down ↓

1 Who takes the lessons in school?
2 It's very late. I must go _____ bed.
3 The match will start _____ 3 p.m.
5 (*See picture*.)
7 This is a television _____. (*See also picture*.)
8 There are two _____ on this horse. (*See also picture*.)
9 What did you eat for breakfast? I _____ an egg.
10 Coming to the end of life.
11 (*See picture*.)
12 This man is very _____. (*See also picture*.)
13 Very bad pains.
15 What noise do cows make?
20 Peter is climbing _____ the stairs. (*See also picture*.)
21 Short for 'Doctor'.

2 →

5 ↓

4 →

7 ↓

16 →

8 ↓

11 ↓

18 →

12 ↓

20 ↓

Across →

4 (*See picture.*)
5 (*See picture.*)
7 What is this woman carrying? (*See also picture.*)
8 Can you _____ a picture?
9 Sand will _____ at the bottom of the sea.
12 When they stop beating, we die.
14 Tom plays football. He _____ plays golf.
15 The colour of blood.
16 (*See picture.*)
17 Mary is seven. Jane is eight. They are different _____ .

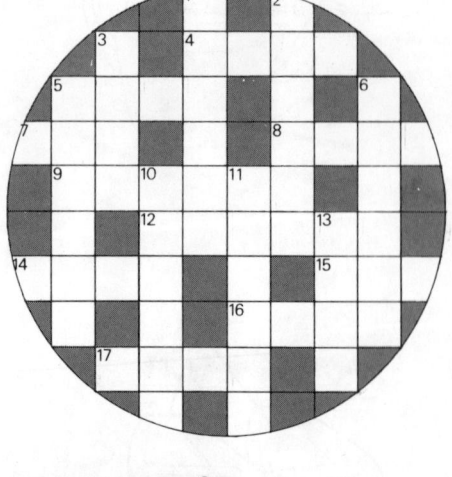

Down ↓

1 Make something.
2 (*See picture.*)
3 This puzzle is on _____ 24.
5 A big, strong house where a king lives.
6 A bucket _____ water in a well.
10 Even _____ I tried, I couldn't lift it.
11 Have you heard the _____ news?
13 (*See picture.*)

4 ⇨

5 ⇨

7 ⇨

16 ⇨

2 ⬇
13 ⬇
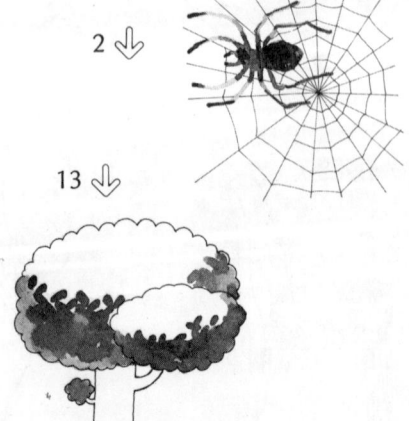

Across →

1 (*See picture.*)
7 An _____ machine works on its own.
8 Engines _____ coaches on the railway.
9 (*See picture.*)
12 It shows you when trains come and go.
14 When I'm happy, I'm in high _____ .

Down ↓

2 Do you know a good _____ where I can stay?
3 My friends _____ to my house yesterday.
4 What would you like to _____ for tea?
5 (*See picture.*)
6 Jim has _____ the top of the bottle on. (*See also picture.*)
10 If you don't wash your hands, it's a bad _____ .
11 Here's a spoon to _____ your coffee. (*See also picture.*)
13 (*See picture.*)

1 ⇨

9 ⇨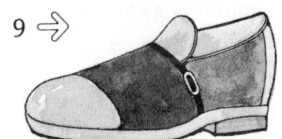

5 ⇩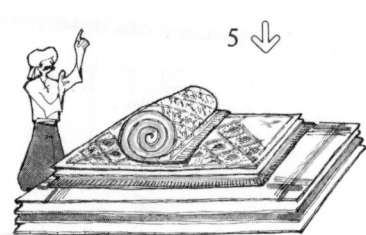

6 ⇩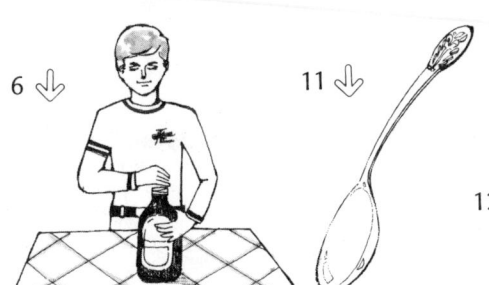

11 ⇩

13 ⇩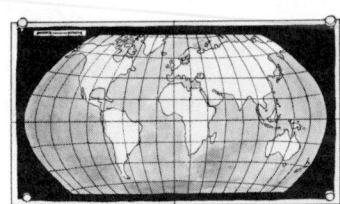

Across →

1 (*See picture.*)
3 _____ can you tell me the time?
5 (*See picture.*)
6 I'm not hungry. I don't want anything to _____ .
8 Everything in the world and in space.
9 Have you _____ the new film?
10 The meat of a young cow when you eat it.
11 Elizabeth is _____ at the table. (*See also picture.*)

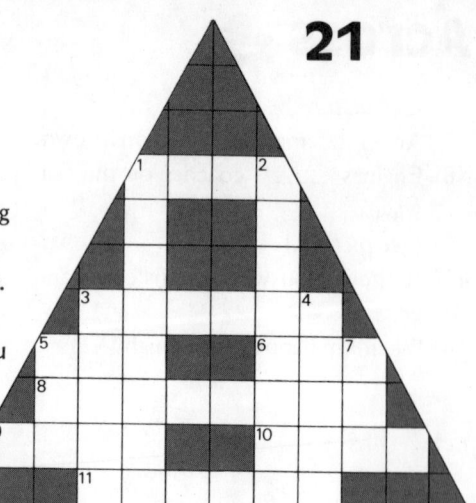

Down ↓

1 Where coal is dug out of the ground.
2 Keep something carefully.
3 These are _____ of glass. (*See also picture.*)
4 Made more easy.
5 We are _____ to meet tomorrow.
7 A cup of _____ . (*See also picture.*)

Across →

22

1 (*See picture.*)
3 What animal gives us ham?
5 My mother cooks by _____.
6 This is Michael's father. Michael is his _____ . (*See also picture.*)
7 Speaks about something.
9 Tear something.
10 What sort of fish is this? (*See also picture.*)
11 What word means a musical instrument and a part of the body?
12 How many toes do you have on both feet? (*See also picture.*)
13 Is Tim chewing _____? (*See also picture.*)
14 When you have read all of a book, you come to the _____ .
15 I walked, but you _____ . You were quicker than me.

Down ↓

1 (*See picture.*)
2 Because it's raining, the game has been _____ until next week.
3 There is one _____ in this car, besides the driver. (*See also picture.*)
4 This picture shows a lady and a _____ . (*See also picture.*)
8 (*See picture.*)

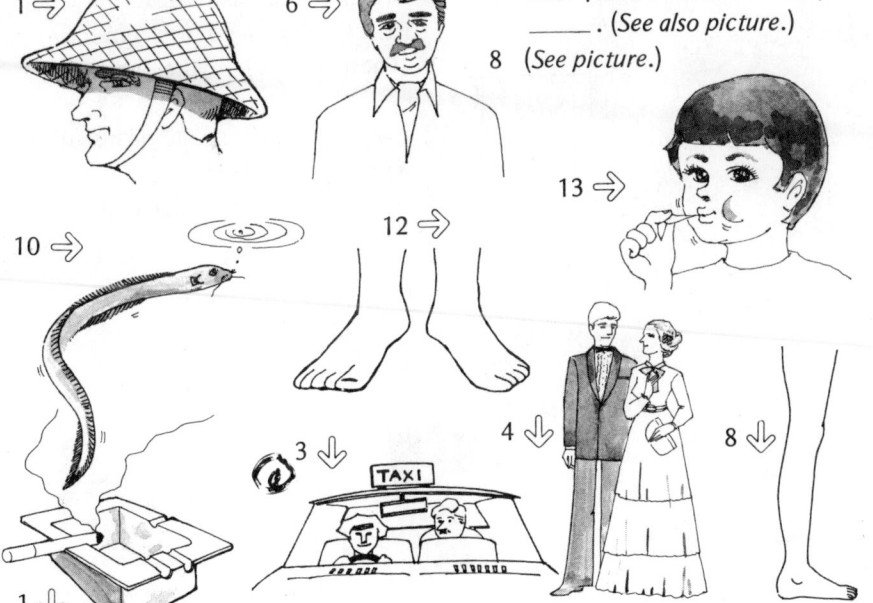

Across →

1   This field is _____ . Keep out!
7   (*See picture.*)
8   In _____ , countries fight each other.
9   If you owe money, you are in _____ .
11 What colour is the sky when there are no clouds?
13 This is neither Dick _____ Bob. It is Harry. (*See also picture.*)
14 Oh dear! Susan has _____ the water jug. (*See also picture.*)
16 Try to do something.

7 ⇨

13 ⇨

Down ↓

2   Steal things from someone.
3   What a beautiful _____ ! (*See also picture.*)
4   (*See picture.*)
5   Martin is a _____ at the university.
6   When a policeman catches a thief, he _____ him. (*See also picture.*)
10 The paper fell in the fire and was _____ .
12 Jack is playing a _____ on his guitar. (*See also picture.*)
15 Take a little drink of something.

14 ⇨

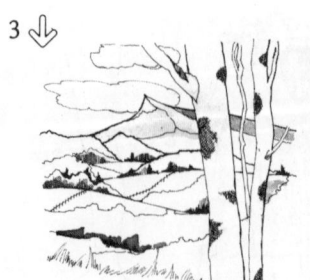

4 ⇩

3 ⇩

6 ⇩

12 ⇩

28

Across ➡️

1 (*See picture.*)
6 A good child _____ his parents.
7 ✓
8 (*See picture.*)
9 A person who tells lies.
10 (*See picture.*)
12 Very surprised about something.

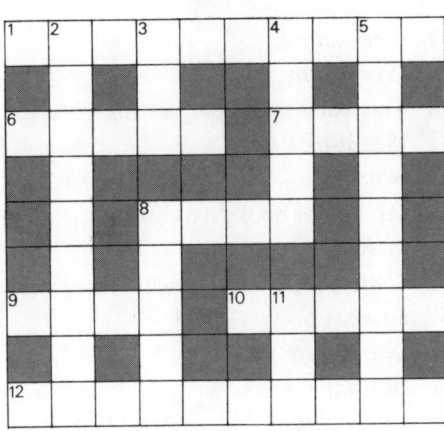

1 ➡️

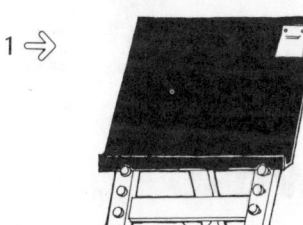

8 ➡️

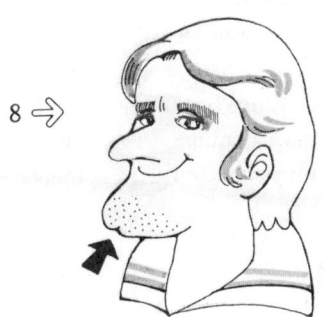

10 ➡️

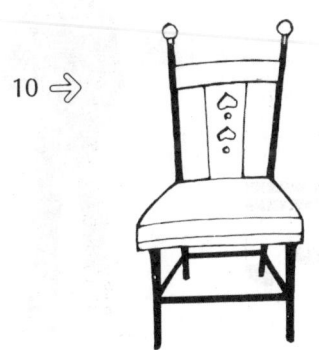

Down ⬇️

2 Places where there are a lot of books to read.
3 What has made Lucy _____? (*See also picture.*)
4 I _____ go to the cinema because I like films.
5 See something and know what it is.
8 All the things a ship takes from one place to another.
11 George _____ taken my pencil.

3 ⬇️

Across →

25

1 (*See picture.*)
4 (*See picture.*)
6 This baby is sleeping in his _____. (*See also picture.*)
7 Not tight.
8 My school books have many _____ in them.
10 Some people _____ while they are asleep.
11 (*See picture.*)
12 Not wet.
13 (*See picture.*)

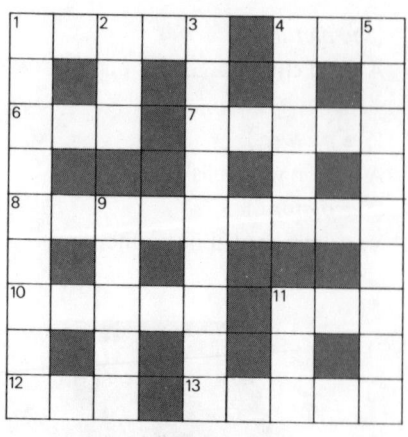

Down ↓

1 Did very well at something.
2 Take a part in a play.
3 (*See picture.*)
4 Puzzle number 8 is in the shape of a _____ .
5 Music is one of the _____ of life.
9 We have a holiday _____ summer.
11 A knife is used to _____ things.

1 ⇒

4 ⇒

11 ⇒

3 ⇓

6 ⇒

13 ⇒

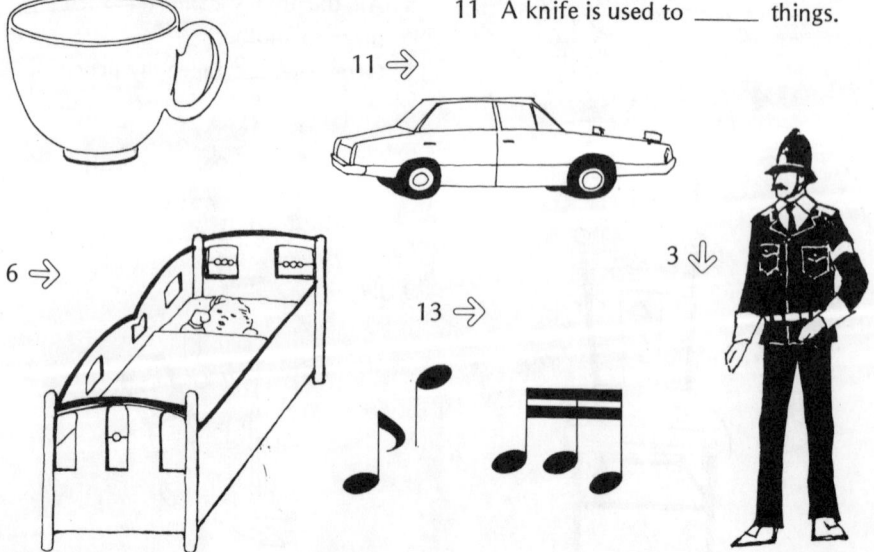

Across →

1 When does the bus come? Look in the
   _____ .

5 (*See picture.*)
6 I like walking long _____ .
10 Someone who lives in Germany.
11 Turn English into German, perhaps.

Down ↓

1 Mary looks very _____ . (*See also pic-ture.*)
2 This snail _____ very slowly. (*See also picture.*)
3 Says bad things to make you scared.
4 Not small.
7 The outer ring is black. The _____ is white. (*See also picture.*)
8 What sign is this?
9 I haven't seen you _____ last year.

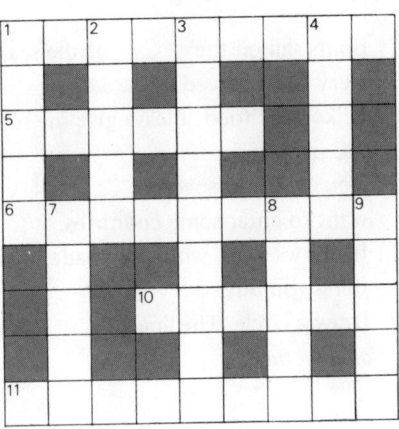

1 ↓

5 ⇒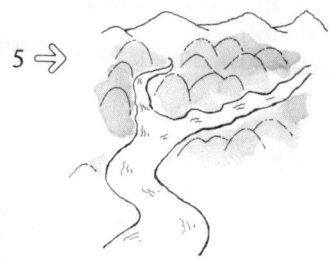

7 ↓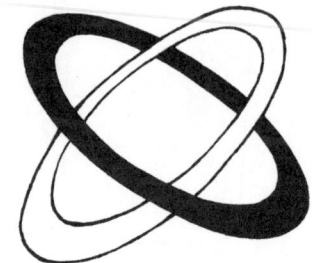

2 ↓

Across →

27

1 Boats sail on the _____ of the sea.
7 Very good indeed.
8 I like that food. Please give me some
   _____ .
9 You need a special _____ if you
   want to enter some countries.
11 It shows you who has made something you buy.
12 Draw a circle. The line is _____ . (*See
   also picture.*)

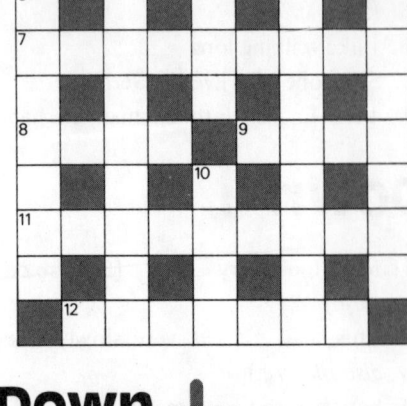

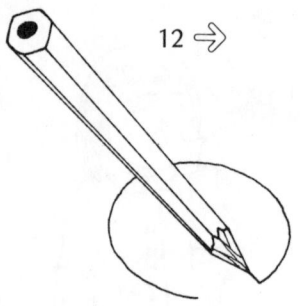

12 ⇨

Down ↓

2 Not sure about something.
3 This glass is _____ of water. (*See also
   picture.*)
4 You learn about them in chemistry.
5 Allows.
6 In war, one country often _____
   another one.
10 (*See picture.*)

3 ⇩

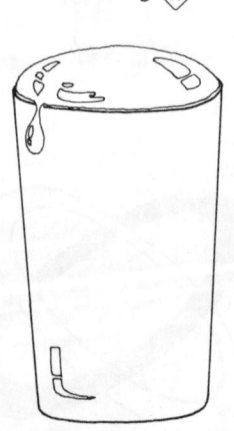

10 ⇩

Across →

1 Given a prize for doing something good.
5 Can you tell me the _____ of the match? Who won?
6 I hope this man will _____ me a lift in his car. (*See also picture.*)
7 Go _____ ! I don't want you here!
9 A bad pain.
10 Susan sings badly. Jane sings worse. Mary sings _____ of all.
11 (*See picture.*)
12 Today is Friday, so tomorrow will be _____ .

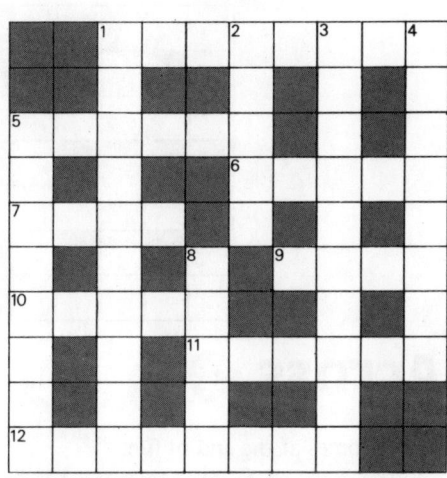

6 ⇒

Down ↓

1 Place where people go out for a meal.
2 (*See picture.*)
3 Something that makes a thing hard to do.
4 Being dear.
5 People walk on pathways. Cars drive on _____ .
8 (*See picture.*)

11 ⇒

2 ⇓

8 ⇓

33

29

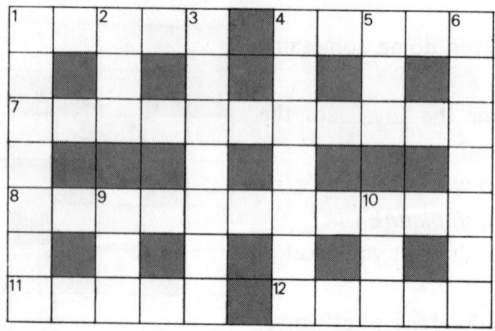

Across →

1 It comes at the end of life.
4 If you want to play, you must wait until _____ school.
7 Makes stronger.
8 The roots of this tree are _____ . (*See also picture*.)
11 If you cut your finger, it will _____ .
12 (*See picture*.)

Down ↓

1 Don't _____ me. I'm trying to work.
2 It's all around us, and we breathe it.
3 100.
4 Changed.
5 (*See picture*.)
6 Lives or stays in a place.
9 Helen wants to _____ her dress to make it a different colour.
10 Life is full of _____ and downs.

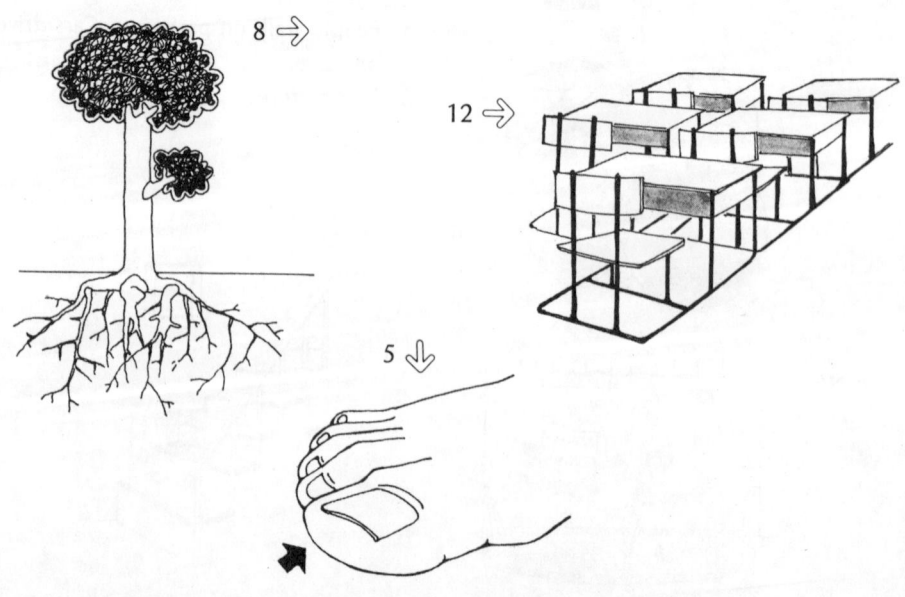

8 ⇒

12 ⇒

5 ⇓

Across →

1 These are _____ lights. (*See also picture.*)
6 We go to the _____ to see plays.
7 People who use cars are called _____ .
9 Strong feeling, like love.
11 Very unusual.

Down ↓

1 What's _____ time? It's four o'clock. (*See also picture.*)
2 It's not four o'clock in the morning, but four o'clock in the _____ .
3 Wool _____ soft when you touch it.
4 These men are _____ the bridge. (*See also picture.*)
5 (*See picture.*)
8 Bill and John are Vicky's brothers. Vicky is _____ sister. (*See also picture.*)
10 On a hot day, put _____ in your drink.

30

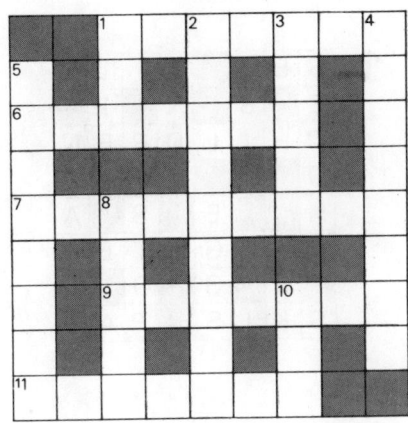

4 ↓

1 ⇒

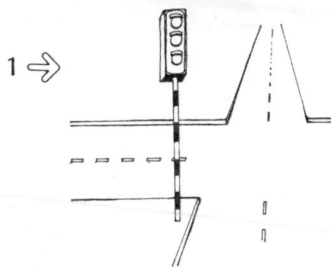

5 ↓

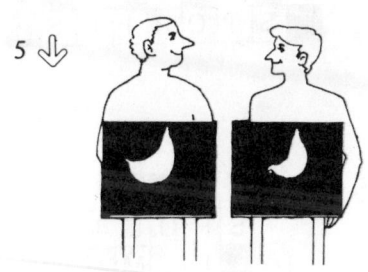

1 ↓

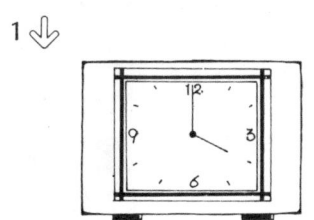

8 ↓

35

Solutions

1
```
S E A · L I L Y
E · S · A · I ·
C H I L D R E N
O · A · Y · E ·
N · · E · S E A
D A U G H T E R
· S · G · O · L
S K I S · P A Y
```

2
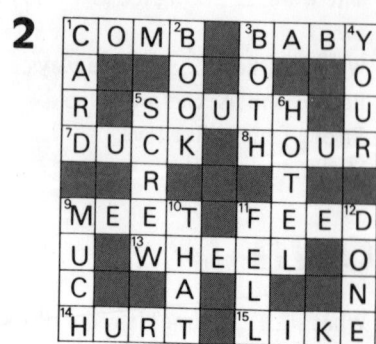
```
C O M B · B A B Y
A · O · O · · · O
R · S O U T H · U
D U C K · H O U R
· R · · · T · · ·
M E E T · · F E E D
U · W H E E L · O
C · A · · L · · N
H U R T · L I K E
```

3
```
· A M E R I C A
L I L I A · S ·
I · L · C A T C H
B · E · H · · H ·
R O S E · W H E N
A · · S · O · I ·
R I G H T · R U N
Y · E · A · · S ·
· S T O R I E S
```

4
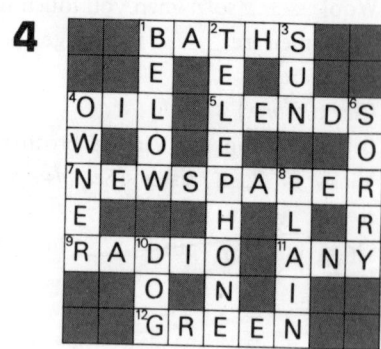
```
· · B A T H S ·
· · E · E · U ·
O I L · L E N D S
W · O · E · S · S
N E W S P A P E R
E · · · H · L · R
R A D I O · A N Y
· · O · N · I · ·
· · G R E E N · ·
```

5
```
· · T · D · ·
· S H O U T ·
A · E · M · A
· C R Y · B O X
S E E · · F · W
E · C · · F · A
C L E V E R E S T
R · I · · R · E
E · V · · E · R
T I E · · D A Y
```

6
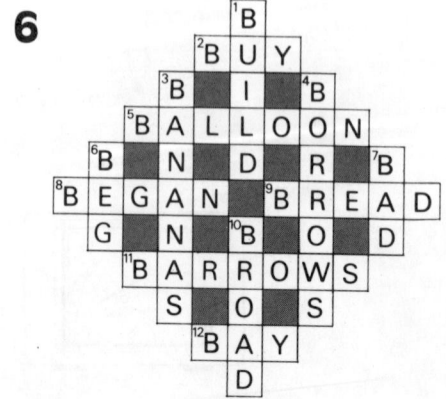
```
· · · B · · ·
· · B U Y · ·
· B · I · B ·
· B A L L O O N
B · N · D · R B
B E G A N · B R E A D
G · N · B · O D
· B A R R O W S
· S · O · S ·
· · B A Y · ·
· · · D · · ·
```

7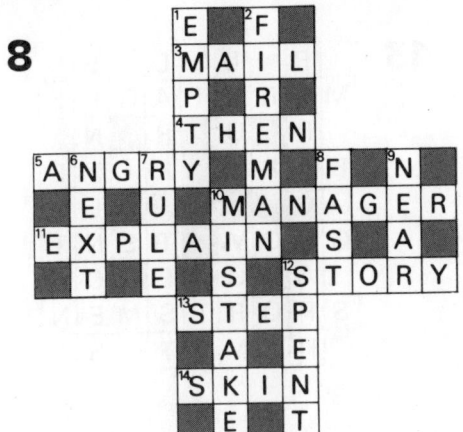

8

9

10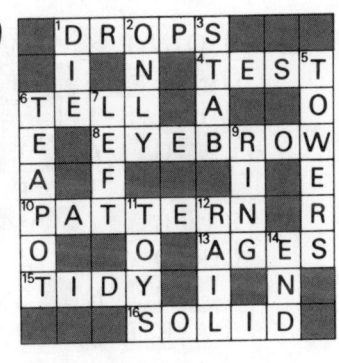

11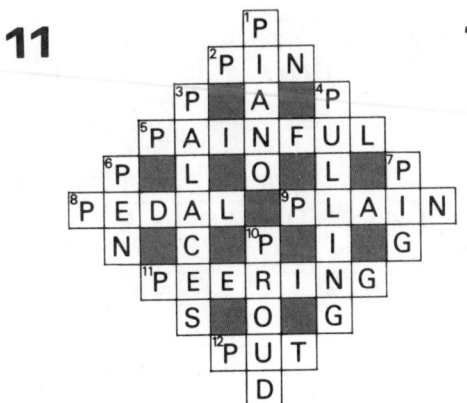

12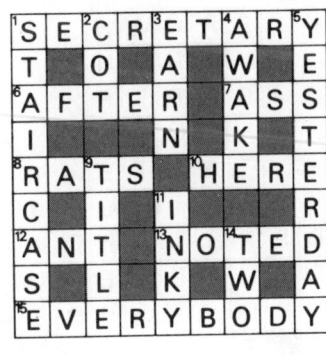

13

```
  P   D   D   S
M A R R I A G E S
  R   U   R   N
F A R M   K I T E
  G           E
G R O W   B E N T
  A   O   E   C
S P O R T S M E N
  H   M   T   S
```

14

```
          S   S
      S A S H
    S K I   I
    S A I L O R S
    S E N D       T         S
  S H E D   S           S U P P L Y
    S W E E T S       S P I N
      I   C I   S I P
    S C H O O L G I R L
      H   N V   L L
    S E E D E   L Y
      S   S P R A Y
```

15

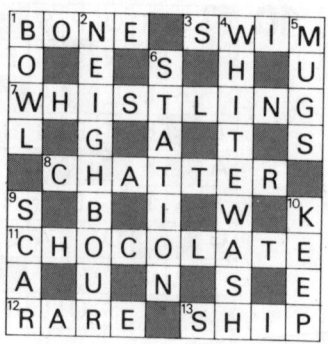

```
B O N E   S W I M
O   E   S   H   U
W H I S T L I N G
L   G   A   T   S
    C H A T T E R
S   B   I   W   K
C H O C O L A T E
A   U   N   S   E
R A R E   S H I P
```

16

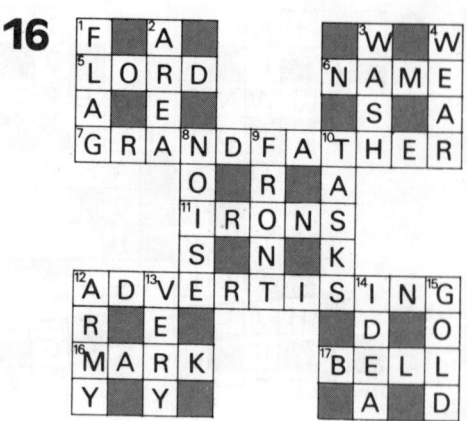

```
F   A       W W
L O R D   N A M E
A   E     S   A
G R A N D F A T H E R
    O   R   A
   I R O N S
    S   N   K
A D V E R T I S I N G
R E           D G
M A R K     B E L L
Y Y           A D
```

17

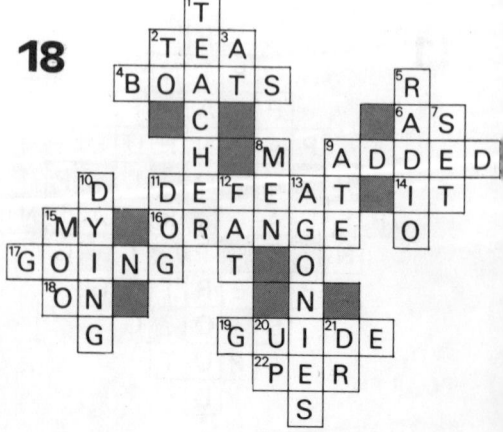

```
B R O W N
U P   U
R I P E R
S O   S
T A S T E
    I
U N D E R S T A N D I N G
N   R   U   E   D   A
C O O K S   C R E A M
L   V   T   K   A   E
E N E M Y   S E L L S
```

18

```
      T
    T E A
  B O A T S       R
      C   A     S
      H   M   A D D E D
D   D E F E A T   I T
M Y   O R A N G E   O
G O I N G   T   O
  N G       N
        G U I D E
        P E R
        S
```

19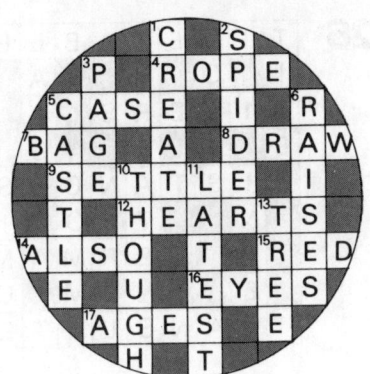

20

21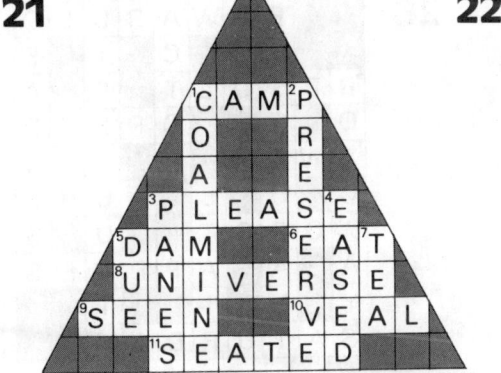

22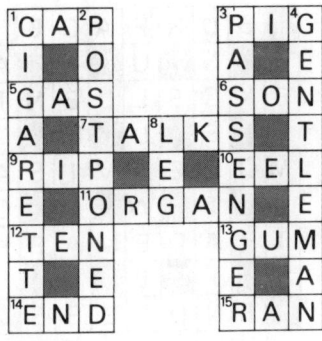

23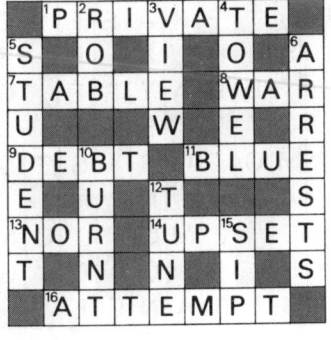

24

25

26

27

	S	U	R	F	A	C	E	
P		N		U		H		A
E	X	C	E	L	L	E	N	T
R		E		L		M		T
M	O	R	E		V	I	S	A
I		T		W		C		C
T	R	A	D	E	M	A	R	K
S		I		L		L		S
	E	N	D	L	E	S	S	

28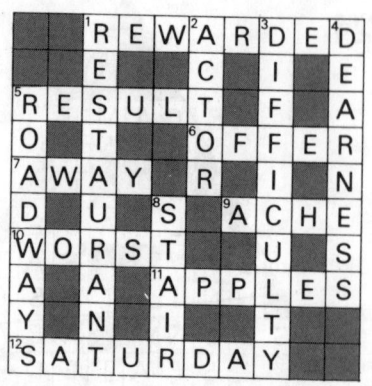

29

D	E	A	T	H		A	F	T	E	R
I		I		U		L		O		E
S	T	R	E	N	G	T	H	E	N	S
T			D		E					I
U	N	D	E	R	G	R	O	U	N	D
R		Y		E		E		P		E
B	L	E	E	D		D	E	S	K	S

30

Word List

A
ace
ache
act
actor
add, added
advertise, advertising
after
afternoon
age, ages
agony, agonies
air
all
also
alter, altered
America
angry
ant
any
apple
area
arm
army
arrest
as
Asia
ask
ass
astonish, astonished
at
attack
attempt
automatic
awake
away
axe

B
baby
bad
bag
balloon
banana
barrow
bath
bay
beg
begin, began
bell
below
bent
best
blackboard
bleed
blue
boat
bone
book
borrow
both
bowl
box
boy
bread
broad
brown
build
burn, burnt
burst
buy

C
camp
cap
car
card
cargo
carpet
case
castle
cat
catch
chair
chance
chatter
chemical
chicken
child, children
chin
chocolate
cigarette
clever, cleverest
coalmine
comb
come, came
comma
cook
cot
cream
create
cross, crossing
cry
cup
cut

D
dam
dark
daughter
day
dear, dearness
death
debt
defeat
desk
die, dying
difficult, difficulty
distance
disturb
do, done
dog
Dr
draw
dream
drive, drove
drop
drum
dry
duck
due
dumb
dye

E
each
ear
earn
ease, eased
eat, ate
eel
egg
emotion
empty
end
endless
enemy
err
every
everybody
excellent
exercise
expensive
explain
eye
eyebrow

F
fall, fell
farm
fast
fat
feed
feel
few
fireman
flag
free
front
full

41

G
game
gas
gate
gentleman
German
get
go, going
gold
grandfather
green
grow
guide
gum

H
habit
hat
have, has
heart
here
his
horse
hotel
hour
hundred

I
ice
idea
ideal
ill
ink, inky
inner
into
iron
it

K
keep
kite

L
lady
lamp

large
late, latest
left
leg
lend
level
liar
library
lie
like
lily
loose
lord

M
mail
man, men
manager
map
mark
marriage
meet
mile
mistake
moo
more
motorist
mountain
moustache
move
much
mug
my

N
name
near
nearly
neck
neighbour
new
newspaper
next
noise

nor
nose
note, noted
now
nurse

O
obey
offer, offered
often
oil
on
only
opposite
orange
organ
other
owe
owner

P
page
painful
palace
pane
paragraph
passenger
pattern
pay
pedal
peer, peering
pen
per
permit
pet
piano
pig
pin
plain
please
pleasure
policeman
postpone,
    postponed

preserve
private
proud
pull, pulling
put

R
radio
rail
raise
rare
rat
reach
receive
recognize
red
reply
reside
restaurant
result
reward, rewarded
rich
right
ring
rip
ripe, riper
river
roadway
rob
rope
rose
rule
run, ran
rust, rusty

S
sail
sailor
sandwich
sash
Saturday
scar
schoolgirl
screw, screwed

sea	spider	taste	tube
seat, seated	spin	tea	tune
second	spirit	teacher	two
secret	sportsman,	teapot	
secretary	sportsmen	telephone	U
see, seen	spray	tell	uncertain
seed	stab	ten	uncle
sell	stair	test	underground
send	staircase	that	understand,
sentence	stamp	the	understanding
set	star	theatre	universe
settle	station	their	up, ups
sh!	step, stepped	then	upset
shed	stir	they	
shine, shining	stomach	thin	V
ship	stop	though	veal
shirt	story, stories	threaten	very
shoe	strange	tick	view
shout	strengthen	tidy	visa
silly	student	tie	
silver	succeed, succeeded	timetable	W
since	sum	tire, tired	war
sip	sun	title	wash
Sir	supply	to	water, watery
ski	sure	toe	wear
skid	surface	top	well
skin	sweet, sweets	towel	wheel
sleep	swim	tower	when
solid	system	town	whistle, whistling
somewhere		toy	whitewash
son	T	trademark	worm
sorry	table	traffic	worst
south	talk	translate	
spend, spent	task	tree	Y
			yesterday
			you, your

Note: The words within the common-core vocabulary selected for compiling this series are printed in *italic* type in the list above. The complete common-core list appears in the *Introductory* book.